R Programming for Beginners

Fast and Easy Learning R

Table of Contents

Introduction 5

Chapter 1- A Brief Overview of R Programming 6

Chapter 2- Setting up the Environment 7

Chapter 3- Data Types in R 9

Chapter 4- Variables 14

Chapter 5- Decision Making 17

Chapter 6- Loops 21

Chapter 7- Functions 27

Chapter 8- Strings 33

Chapter 9- Vectors 40

Chapter 10- Lists 47

Chapter 11- Matrices 56

Chapter 12- Arrays 58

Chapter 13- Factors 64

Chapter 14- Data Frames 68

Conclusion 71

4

Introduction

In fields dealing with statistical analysis, graphs and charts are widely used. Instead of having to draw and analyze these manually, we should look for alternative ways which will help us automate the process. R is a programming language which can help us in this. It is easy for anyone, even those without a programming background to learn how to program in R. The program has numerous features which we can take advantage of so as to accomplish our tasks in statistical analysis. This book explores these features in detail. Enjoy reading!

Chapter 1- A Brief Overview of R Programming

R is a programming language as well as a software environment used for graphical presentations, statistical analysis, and reporting. It is an interpreted programming language which supports features such as looping, branching, and modular programming by use of functions. It can be integrated with functions which have been written in C, C++, FORTRAN, Python, and .Net programming languages.

Chapter 2- Setting up the Environment

There exist some environments online which have already been setup for you, so feel free to take advantage of them. However, you may also choose to setup your environment on your local machine.

Installation on Windows

Begin by downloading the R, specifically the version for Windows and then save it in your local directory. It will come in an executable form (.exe), so you just have to double click on it and then begin the installation. It is good for you to accept the defaults for the installation to be easy for you. For those using the Windows 32-bit, only the 32-bit version will be installed, while for those using the 6-bit version, both the 32-bit and 6-bit versions of the setup will be installed.

Once the installation has been completed, you can locate the icon and then run it, and you will be presented with the R console from where you can do the programming.

Installation on Linux

Begin by downloading the right version of R for your Linux system. The installation steps vary from distribution to distribution, but you can find these in the provided links. However, for those in R, use the *"yum"* command and install R as shown below:

$ yum install R

With the above command, the R will be installed together with its standard packages, but if you need the core packages, you can launch its console as shown below:

$ R

The prompt will then be presented to you, and you can use the "*install*" command to install any package that you may need. Consider the example given below, which shows how to install a package in R:

> **install("plotrix")**

Consider the example R program given below:

 # Print Hello guys.
print("Hello guys!")
 # Add two numbers.
print(11 + 5)

The above program should give you the output given below:

```
[1] "Hello guys!"
[1] 16
```

That is how a script is written in R. Also, you can write some programs on the R prompt. This is shown below:

```
> hello <- "Hello guys!"
> print(hello)
[1] "Hello guys!"
>
```

Just open the R prompt, and then type the above. The program should give you the output as shown above.

Chapter 3- Data Types in R

Variables are used for the purpose of storing information. They preserve memory locations for the purpose of storing values. Let us discuss how the various data types are defined in R.

Vectors

Whenever you need to create a vector which should have more than one element, then you have to use the function "c()," which is an indication that the elements will be combined into a vector.

Consider the example given below, showing how this can be done:

```
# Create a vector.
student <- c('john','mark',"jane")
print(student)
# Get the class of our vector.
print(class(student))
```

Execution of the above program should give you the following result:

```
[1] "john" "mark" "jane"
[1] "character"
```

Lists

In R, a list is an object which can be used for holding a number of elements such as functions, vectors, and even other lists in it. Consider the example given below:

```
# Create a list.
mylist <- list(c(1,2,3),22.4,sin)
```

# Print the list.
print(mylist)

The program will give you the output shown below:

```
[[1]]
[1] 1 2 3

[[2]]
[1] 22.4

[[3]]
function (x)   .Primitive("sin")
```

Matrices

This is a data set represented in a two-dimensional form. To create a matrix in R, we use a vector input to the matrix function. This is demonstrated below:

# Create a matrix.
M = matrix(c('x','x','y','z','y','x'), nrow = 2, ncol = 3, byrow = TRUE)

print(M)

The program should give you the following output:

```
     [,1] [,2] [,3]
[1,] "x"  "x"  "y"
[2,] "z"  "y"  "x"
```

Arrays

We have said that matrices are in a two-dimensional format. In the case of arrays, any number of dimensions can be used. The array attribute will always go with the *"dim"* attribute which will specify the number of dimensions that you want to create. Consider the example given below in which we will create a two-dimensional array:

 # Create an array.
a <- array(c('boy','girl'),dim = c(3,3,2))
print(a)

The program should give you the output given below:

```
, , 1

        [,1]    [,2]    [,3]
[1,]  "boy"   "girl"  "boy"
[2,]  "girl"  "boy"   "girl"
[3,]  "boy"   "girl"  "boy"

, , 2

        [,1]    [,2]    [,3]
[1,]  "girl"  "boy"   "girl"
[2,]  "boy"   "girl"  "boy"
[3,]  "girl"  "boy"   "girl"
```

Factors

These are R objects which are normally created by the use of vectors. It works by storing the vector together with its distinct values and the elements in our vector such as the labels. The labels are usually in a vector form, regardless of the data type that you are working with. They provide a very important functionality when it comes to statistical modeling.
For us to create factors in C, we have to use the *"factor()"* function._The function *"nlevels"* is used for the purpose of counting the levels. Consider the example given below, which best demonstrates this:

```
# Create a vector.
trouser_colors <-
c('pig','pig','yellow','red','red','red','pig')
# Create a factor object.
factor_trouser <- factor(trouser_colors)
# Print the factor.
print(factor_trouser)
print(nlevels(factor_trouser))
```

Execution of the above program should give out the following
output:

```
[1] pig     pig     yellow red     red     red     pig
Levels: pig red yellow
[1] 3
```

Data Frames

These are data objects in a tabular form. Each column in a data frame can have a different mode of data, which is not the case with matrices. For us to create a data frame in R, we have to use the function *"data.frame()."* Consider the example given below:

```
# Create the data frame.
DF <-        data.frame(
  gender = c("Male", "Male","Female"),
  height = c(120, 123.5, 150),
  weight = c(41,72, 58),
  Age = c(31,26,12)
)
print(DF)
```

The program should give you the following output when executed:

```
  gender height weight Age
1   Male  120.0     41  31
2   Male  123.5     72  26
3 Female  150.0     58  12
```

Chapter 4- Variables

These always provide us with a named storage, and our programs are in a position to manipulate this. For a variable name to be valid in R, it has to be made up of letters, numbers, and the underscore character. The name cannot start with a number.

Variable Assignment

The leftward, rightward, and equal operators can be used for assigning values to variables. To print the value of the variable, you can use the *"print()"* or the *"cat()"* function. The *"cat()"* function will combine the multiple items so as to get a continuous output. Consider the example given below, which best demonstrates this:

```
#  using equal operator for assignment
var.1 = c(5,6,7,8)
# using leftward operator for assignment
var.2 <- c("learn programming in","R")
# using rightward operator for assignment
c(TRUE,1) -> var.3
print(var.1)
cat ("var.1 is ", var.1 ,"\n")
cat ("var.2 is ", var.2 ,"\n")
cat ("var.3 is ", var.3 ,"\n")
```

The program will print the following output when executed:

```
[1] 5 6 7 8
var.1 is   5 6 7 8
var.2 is   learn programming in R
var.3 is   1 1
```

Data Type for a Variable

Variables are not declared to be of a particular data type in R. What happens is that it will get the data type of the R object already assigned to it. This is why R is a dynamically typed language, meaning that the data type of the variable can be changed again and again in our program. Consider the example given below:

```
var_y <- "Hello"
cat("The class for var_y is ",class(var_y),"\n")
var_y <- 34.5
cat(" At this point, the class for var_y is
",class(var_y),"\n")

var_x <- 27L
cat(" Lastly, the class for var_y becomes
",class(var_y),"\n")
```

The program will give the following output after execution:

```
The class for var_y is   character
   At this point, the class for var_y is   numeric
     Lastly, the class for var_y becomes   numeric
```

Finding Variables

The "*ls()*" is used for the purpose of listing all of the variables which are contained in our workspace. It can also be used with patterns for the purpose of matching the names of variables. This is shown below:

print(ls())

The above program should give you all of the variables which have been defined in your workspace. Note that if you have none, then nothing will be printed out. Also, note that the variables have to match the ones you have defined within your programming environment.

15

The command can be used as follows with patterns:

 # List variables starting with pattern "var".
print(ls(pattern = "var"))

Deleting Variables

The "*rm()*" function can be used for the purpose of deleting variables. Suppose that we are in need of deleting a variable with the name "*var.2.*" This can be done as shown in the code given below:

rm(var.2)
print(var.2)

The "*ls()*" and "*rm()*" functions can be used for the purpose of deleting functions at the same time. This is shown below:

rm(list = ls())
print(ls())

Chapter 5- Decision Making

These require that the programmer should set some conditions which are to be evaluated, and the statements which are to be expected based on whether the condition is true or false. Let us discuss the decision-making statements which are supported in R programming language:

"If" Statement

This is made up of a Boolean expression, which is then followed by one or more statements. The statement takes the syntax given below:

```
if(boolean_expression) {
   // statement(s) to be executed if the boolean
expression evaluates to true.
}
```

If the set condition is found to be true, then the statements inside the curly brace will be executed, while in case it evaluates to a *"false,"* then the statements immediately after the *"if"* statement will be executed. Consider the example given below showing how this can be used:

```
y <- 30L
if(is.integer(y)) {
   print("Y is an Integer")
}
```

On execution, the program will give you the following output:

```
[1] "Y is an Integer"
```

"If...Else" Statement

This is made up of an "*if*" statement, which is followed by an optional "*else*" statement which will be executed if the condition is found to be "*false.*" It takes the syntax given below:

if(boolean_expression) {
   // statement(s) to execute if the boolean expression evaluates to true.

} else {
   // statement(s) to execute if the boolean expression evaluates to false.

}

If the condition evaluates to a true, the statements within the "*if*" block will be executed, while if the condition evaluates to a "*false,*" then the statements within the "*else*" block will be executed. The example given below shows how this works:

y <- c("what","was","truth")
if("Truth" %in% y) {
   print("Truth was found")
} else {
   print("Truth was not found")
}

Execution of the above program will give you the following output:

```
[1] "Truth was not found"
```

The "if...else if...else" Statement

This involves an *"if"* statement which is then followed by an optional *"else...if...else"* statement which is very good for a number of conditions. This takes the basic syntax given below:

```
if(boolean_expression 1) {
   // will execute once the boolean expression 1
evaluates to true.
} else if( boolean_expression 2) {
   // will execute once the boolean expression 2
evaluates to true.
} else if( boolean_expression 3) {
   // will execute once the boolean expression 3
evaluates to true.
} else {
   // will execute once none of the above condition
evaluates to true.

}
```

This is demonstrated in the code given below:

```
y <- c("what","was","truth")
if("Truth" %in% y) {
   print("Truth was found on the first time")
} else if ("truth" %in% y) {
   print("truth was found on the second time")
} else {
   print("No truth was found")
}
```

Execution of the above program will give the following output:

```
[1] "truth was found on the second time"
```

Switch Statement

This will allow a particular variable to be tested against a list of some other values. Each value is referred to as a *"case,"* and the variable which is to be switched has to be checked for each case which exists.

The statement takes the syntax given below:

switch(expression, case1, case2, case3....)

Consider the example given below; which best demonstrates how this can be done:

```
y <- switch(
  1,
  "first",
  "second",
  "third",
  "fourth"
)
print(y)
```

The program should give you the following output once executed:

```
[1] "first"
```

Chapter 6- Loops

Sometimes, one needs to execute a particular block of code for a number of times. In this case, the statements will have to be executed in a sequential manner, meaning that the first statement is executed, followed by the second, and so on. The following are the types of loops which are supported in the R programming language.

Repeat Loop

With this loop, a piece of code of code will be executed again and again until it finds a stop condition. The repeat loop in R takes the following syntax:

```
repeat {
  commands
  if(condition) {
    break
  }
}
```

Consider the example given below, which shows how this loop can be used:

```
hl <- c("Hello","guys!")
cnt <- 2
repeat {
  print(hl)
  cnt <- cnt+1
  if(cnt > 5) {
    break
  }
}
```

Execution of the above program will give you the following output:

```
[1] "Hello"  "guys!"
[1] "Hello"  "guys!"
[1] "Hello"  "guys!"
[1] "Hello"  "guys!"
```

While Loop

This type of loop will execute the same code again and again until it means a particular condition. The loop takes the syntax given below:

while (test_expression) {
  statement
}

With such syntax, the loop might end up not running. If after testing the condition it is found to be false, the loop will have to be skipped, and then the condition which first occurs after the loop will be executed. The example given below shows how this happens:

hl <- c("Hello","this is a while loop")
cnt <- 2
while (cnt < 6) {
  print(hl)
  cnt = cnt + 1
}

Execution of the above program should give you the following as the output:

```
[1] "Hello"          "this is a while loop"
[1] "Hello"          "this is a while loop"
[1] "Hello"          "this is a while loop"
[1] "Hello"          "this is a while loop"
```

For Loop

This is a repetition control structure which will help you in writing a loop allowing you to execute a particular section of code for a specific number of times. The statement takes the basic syntax given below:

for (value in vector) {
  statements
}

These loops are very flexible, since they have not been limited to numbers or even numbers as the input. We are in a position to pass logical vectors, character vectors, and expressions or lists. Consider the example given below which shows how this type of loop can be used:

l <- LETTERS[1:5]
for (j in l) {
  print(j)
}

Execution of the above program will give you the following output:

```
[1]  "A"
[1]  "B"
[1]  "C"
[1]  "D"
[1]  "E"
```

Loop Control Statements

These statements will change the process of execution from the normal sequence. Once the scope of execution is left, the automatic objects which had been created in that scope will be destroyed. Let us discuss the control statements which are supported in the R programming language.

Break Statement

This statement has the following two uses in the R programming language:

- When the statement is found inside a loop, the loop will be terminated immediately, and then the program control will resume in the next statement which follows the loop.

- We can use the break statement to terminate a case contained in a switch statement.

The statement takes the following syntax:

Break

Consider the example given below, which shows how the statement can be used:

```
hl <- c("Hello","guys!")
cnt <- 2
repeat {
  print(hl)
  cnt <- cnt + 1

  if(cnt > 6) {
    break
  }
}
```

Execution of the above program should give the following output:

```
[1]  "Hello"  "guys!"
[1]  "Hello"  "guys!"
[1]  "Hello"  "guys!"
[1]  "Hello"  "guys!"
[1]  "Hello"  "guys!"
```

Next Statement

This statement is very important in R when we need to skip the iteration on the current loop without having to terminate it. When the R interpreter encounters this statement in the program, it will skip any further evaluation and then start the next iteration of our loop. The statement takes the following syntax:

Next

Consider the example shown below, which shows how this statement can be used in R:

```
l <- LETTERS[1:6]
for ( j in l) {

  if (j == "C") {
    next
  }
  print(j)
}
```

Execution of the program should give you the following as the output:

```
[1]  "A"
[1]  "B"
[1]  "D"
[1]  "E"
[1]  "F"
```

Chapter 7- Functions

This represents a set of statements which have been grouped together for the purpose of performing a specific task. There are a number of built-in functions in R, and the user is allowed to create his functions.

R sees functions as objects, meaning that the R interpreter will be in a position to pass control to the function, together with the arguments which may be good for the function to accomplish its tasks. The function will then perform its tasks and then pass control to the interpreter and the results which might have been stored in the other functions.

Definition of functions in R is done by use of the *"function"* keyword. It takes the syntax shown below:

function_name <- function(argument_1, argument_2, ...) {

  Function body
}

The following are the different parts of the function:
1. Function Name- this represents the actual name of the function. It is stored as an object with that name in the R environment.

2. Arguments- this is just a placeholder. Once the function has been invoked, a value will then be passed into the argument. The arguments can have default values, but note that the arguments are optional in a function, as functions can be used without arguments.

3. Function Body- this is made up of a collection of statements defining what the function will do.

4. Return value- this is the last expression in our function body which is to be evaluated.

In R, there exist many built-in functions which one can call directly without having to redefine once again.

Built-in Functions in R

Examples of built-in functions in R are mean (), max (),seq(), sum(x), and paste(...). These can easily be called from the user-written programs. Consider the example given below, which shows how these can be used:

 # Creating a sequence of numbers ranging between 31 to 45.

print(seq(31,45))
 # Find the mean of the numbers from 20 to 62.
print(mean(20:62))
 # Finding the sum of the numbers between 40 to 69.
print(sum(40:69))

Executing the above program will give you the following output:

```
[1] 31 32 33 34 35 36 37 38 39 40 41 42 43 44 45
[1] 41
[1] 1635
```

User-define Function

R allows users to define their own functions. These are specific to what the user needs, and they can be used just like the built-in functions once they have been defined. The example given below shows how to create and use a function in R:

 # Creating a function for printing the squares of the numbers in sequence.

```
new.function <- function(x) {
    for(j in 1:x) {
```

```
  y <-j^2
  print(y)
  }
}
```

We have mentioned a function call. Let us demonstrate how a function is called in R:

 # Creating a function for printing the squares of the numbers in sequence.

```
new.function <- function(x) {
  for(j in 1:x) {
    y <-j^2
    print(y)
  }
}
```
 # Calling the function new.function and supply 5 as an argument.
new.function(5)

Execution of the above program should give you the following output:

```
[1] 1
[1] 4
[1] 9
[1] 16
[1] 25
```

Also, it is possible for us to call a function without using an argument. The example given below best demonstrates this:

 # Creating a function with no argument.
new.function <- function() {
  for(j in 1:5) {
    print(j^2)
  }
}

 # Calling the function with no argument.
new.function()

Execution of the above program should give you the following output:

```
[1] 1
[1] 4
[1] 9
[1] 16
[1] 25
```

The argument values can be used to call a function, both by their position and name. This means that the arguments have to be supplied in the same order that they were defined in the function, or maybe supplied in a different sequence but assigned by use of their names. Consider the example given below, which best demonstrates this:

 # Creating a function with the arguments.
new.function <- function(x,y,z) {
  result <- x * y + z
  print(result)
}
 # Calling the function by the position of arguments.
new.function(4,3,12)
 # Calling the function by the names of arguments.
new.function(x = 10, y = 7, z = 2)

Execution of the above program should give out the following output:

```
[1] 24
[1] 72
```

Also, we can make use of default arguments so as to call our function. We can then call our function without supplying any arguments, and this will give us the default result. At the same time, we can pass in new values, and this will allow us to get another result rather than the default one. Consider the example given below showing how this can be done:

```
# Creating a function with some arguments.
new.function <- function(x = 2, y = 6) {
   result <- x * y
   print(result)
}
# Calling the function with no giving any argument.
new.function()
# Calling the function with giving some new values for
the argument.

new.function(7,5)
```

Executing the above program will give you the following output:

```
[1]  12
[1]  35
```

31

Lazy Evaluation of a Function

The arguments to our functions have to be evaluated lazily, meaning that we only execute them when the function body needs them. The example given below best demonstrates how this can be done:

 # Creating a function with some arguments.
new.function <- function(x, y) {
  print(x^2)
  print(x)
  print(y)
}
 # Evaluating the function with no supplying one of arguments.
new.function(8)

Execution of the above program should give you the result given below:

```
[1] 64
[1] 8
Error in print(y) : argument "y" is missing, with no default
Calls: new.function -> print
Execution halted
```

Chapter 8- Strings

In R, strings are written within single or double quotes. Although you are allowed to use single quotes for declaration of a string in R, these are internally with double quotes. Note that you are not allowed to mix the quotes, that is, you should use either single quotes at the start and end of the string or double quotes at the start and end of the string. Mixing the two will cause an error. However, if you have started and ended with single quotes, it is possible for you to insert double quotes within the string. The same case applies to a string which starts and ends with single quotes, as you are allowed to insert single quotes within. Even though that is true, you are not allowed to insert double quotes inside a string which starts and ends with double quotes. The same case applies when you are using single quotes.

Consider the example given below which shows how these can be used:

w <- 'Begin and end with a single quote'
print(w)
x <- "Begin and end with the double quotes"
print(x)
y <- "single quote ' added in between the double quotes"
print(y)
z <- 'Double quotes " added in between sa ingle quote'
print(z)

Above are examples of some valid strings in R programming language? Execution of the program should give you the result given below:

```
[1] "Begin and end with a single quote"
[1] "Begin and end with the double quotes"
[1] "single quote ' added in between the double quotes"
[1] "Double quotes \" added in between sa ingle quote"
```

Consider the example below, which shows some invalid strings in R:

```
x <- 'Mixed quotes"
print(x)
y <- 'Single quote ' inside a single quote'
print(y)
z <- "Double quotes " inside other double quotes"
print(z)
```

Execution of the program will give you the following result:

```
Error: unexpected symbol in:
"print(x)
y <- 'Single"
Execution halted
```

String Manipulation

Concatenation or combination of strings in R is done by use of the *"paste()"* function. This function is ready to take any number of arguments which you need to concatenate. The syntax for this is given below:

paste(..., sep = " ", collapse = NULL)

The "..." is used for representation of the number of arguments which are to be combined or concatenated. The *"sep"* is used for representing any separator between our arguments, but this one is optional. The *"collapse"* is used for eliminating any space in two strings. However, this is not the space existing between any two words of a string.

Consider the example given below:

```
x <- "Hi"
y <- 'How'
z <- "was your day? "
print(paste(x,y,z))
print(paste(x,y,z, sep = "-"))
print(paste(x,y,z, sep = "", collapse = ""))
```

Execution of the program should give you the following result:

```
[1] "Hi How was your day? "
[1] "Hi-How-was your day? "
[1] "HiHowwas your day? "
```

Sometimes, we may need to format our strings and numbers so as to get a specific style. This can be done by use of the *"format()"* function.

Below is the basic syntax for this function:

35

**format(x, digits, nsmall, scientific, width, justify =
c("left", "right", "centre", "none"))**

The following parameters have been used in the above syntax:
1. x- this represents our vector input.

2. digits- this is the total number of digits which are to be displayed.

3. nsmall- this is the minimum number of digits which can be accepted on the right side of the decimal point.

4. scientific- this has to be set to true for the purpose of displaying the scientific notation.

5. width- this will indicate the minimum width which is to be displayed by our padding blocks at the beginning.

6. justify- this refers to the display of our string to the right, left, or center.

Consider the example given below, which shows how these parameters can be used:

 # Total number of digits to be displayed. The last digit has been rounded off.

```
result <- format(11.123456789, digits = 9)
print(result)
# Display the numbers in a scientific notation.
result <- format(c(6, 19.13761), scientific = TRUE)
print(result)
# The minimum number of the digits to right of our
decimal point.

result <- format(34.46, nsmall = 5)
print(result)
```

```
# Formating will treat everything as a string.
result <- format(6)
print(result)
# Numbers padded with blank in beginning for the
width.
result <- format(15.7, width = 6)
print(result)
# Left justify strings.
result <- format("Hello", width = 8, justify = "l")
print(result)
# Justfying the string with center.
result <- format("Hello", width = 8, justify = "c")
print(result)
```

Execution of the above program should give you the following result:

```
[1] "11.1234568"
[1] "6.000000e+00" "1.913761e+01"
[1] "34.46000"
[1] "6"
[1] "   15.7"
[1] "Hello   "
[1] " Hello  "
```

It is also possible for us to count the number of characters which our string has. This is done by use of the *"nchar()"* function. The function will count the number of characters which our string has, including the white spaces. It takes the basic syntax given below:

nchar(x)

In which the *"x"* is a vector input.

Consider the example given below, showing how this function can be used in R programming:

result <- nchar("Counting number of characters")
print(result)

Execution of the program should give the result given below:

```
[1] 29
```

29 is the number of characters in our string, including the spaces.

It is also possible for us to play around with the strings by changing the case, that is, from uppercase to lowercase and vice versa. The functions for doing this take the syntax given below:

toupper(x)
tolower(x)

In which the "x" is a vector input. Consider the example given below, showing how these two functions can be used:

 # Change to Upper case.
result <- toupper("This is To Be Changed To UpperCase")
print(result)
 # Change to lower case.
result <- tolower("This is To Be Changed To Lowercase")
print(result)

Execution of the above program should give you the result given below:

```
[1] "THIS IS TO BE CHANGED TO UPPERCASE"
[1] "this is to be changed to lowercase"
```

It is also possible for us to extract parts of a string. This is done by use of the *"substring()"* function, which takes the syntax given below:

substring(x,first,last)

The following parameters have been used in the above syntax:
1. x- this represents the character vector input.

2. first- this represents the position of the first character which is to be extracted.

3. last- this is the position of the last character which is to be extracted.

Consider the example given below, showing how this function can be used in R:

 # Extracting the characters from 4th to 6th position.
result <- substring("Nicholas", 4, 6)
print(result)

Execution of the program should give you the following result:

```
[1] "hol"
```

Chapter 9- Vectors

These form the most basic data type in the R programming language. There are six types of atomic vectors in R. These include character, integer, double, logical, complex, and raw.

Creating Vectors
Single Element Vector

Once you have written a value in R, it becomes a vector, and it is assigned to any of the above vectors we have discussed. Consider the example given below, which shows how this can be done:

```
# Atomic vector of the character type.
print("xyz");
# Atomic vector of double type.
print(20.5)
# Atomic vector of integer type.
print(72L)
# Atomic vector of logical type.
print(TRUE)
# Atomic vector of complex type.
print(4+2i)
# Atomic vector of raw type.
print(charToRaw('hello'))
```

Execution of the program should give you the output given below:

```
[1] "xyz"
[1] 20.5
[1] 72
[1] TRUE
[1] 4+2i
[1] 68 65 6c 6c 6f
```

Multiple Elements Vector

The colon operator can be used with the numeric data. Consider the example shown below:

 # Create a sequence from 4 to 12.
s <- 4:12
print(s)
 # Create a sequence from 5.6 to 11.6.
s <- 6.6:12.6
print(s)
 # If the finally specified element does not belong to sequence, then it will be discarded.

s <- 3.8:11.4
print(s)

Execution of the program should give the following result:

```
[1]   4   5   6   7   8   9  10  11  12
[1]   6.6   7.6   8.6   9.6  10.6  11.6  12.6
[1]   3.8   4.8   5.8   6.8   7.8   8.8   9.8  10.8
```

The sequence (Seq.) operator can be used as shown below:

 # Creating a vector with the elements from 4 to 8 incrementing by 0.6.

print(seq(4, 8, by = 0.6))

Execution of the program should give you the following result:

```
[1]  4.0  4.6  5.2  5.8  6.4  7.0  7.6
```

The "*c()*" is also of great importance when we are working with strings in R. When used, the non-character values will be coerced to character type if one of its elements is a vector. Consider the example given below, which shows how this can be used:

The numeric and logical values will be converted to characters.

v <- c('apple','red',4,TRUE)
print(v)

When executed, the program will give the result given below:

```
[1] "apple" "red"   "4"     "TRUE"
```

The indexing property is used for the purpose of accessing the vector elements. We use the [] brackets for indexing purpose. This has to begin from position 1. If a value is given a negative index, then it will be dropped from the result. We can also use TRUE and FALSE, represented by 0 and 1 respectively, for indexing purposes.

Consider the example given below, showing how these can be used in R:

Access the vector elements using their position.
d <- c("Sun","Mon","Tue","Wed","Thurs","Fri","Sat")
u <- d[c(2,4,6)]
print(u)
Access the vector elements using their logical indexing.
l <-
t[c(TRUE,FALSE,FALSE,FALSE,FALSE,TRUE,FALSE)]
print(l)

```
# Access the vector elements using a negative
indexing.
y <- t[c(-2,-5)]
print(y)
# Access the vector elements by use of 0/1 indexing.
x <- t[c(0,0,0,0,0,0,1)]
print(x)
```

Vector Arithmetic

We can subtract, add, multiple, or divide two vectors of the same length so as to get the result as a vector input. Consider the example given below, which shows how these operations can be carried out:

```
# Create two vectors.
x1 <- c(3,4,6,5,1,11)
x2 <- c(4,17,0,7,1,8)

# Vector addition.
add.result <- x1+x2
print(add.result)

# Vector substraction.
sub.result <- x1-x2
print(sub.result)
# Vector multiplication.
multi.result <- x1*x2
print(multi.result)
# Vector division.
divi.result <- x1/x2
print(divi.result)
```

Execution of the above program should give you the result given below:

```
[1]  7 21  6 12  2 19
[1]  -1 -13   6  -2   0   3
[1] 12 68  0 35  1 88
[1] 0.7500000 0.2352941      Inf 0.7142857 1.0000000 1.3750000
```

Vector Element Recycling

In some case, we can apply the above operations to vector elements of unequal length. In such a case, the elements of the shorter vector will be recycled so that the operations can be completed. Consider the example given below, which best demonstrates this:

```
x1 <- c(3,7,4,6,0,17)
x2 <- c(5,10)
add.result <- x1+x2
print(add.result)
sub.result <- x1-x2
print(sub.result)
```

Execution of the above program will give the result given below:

```
[1]  8 17  9 16  5 27
[1] -2 -3 -1 -4 -5  7
```

Sorting Vector Elements

The *"sort()"* function can be used for the purpose of sorting vector elements. Consider the example given below, which shows how this can be done:

```
x <- c(3,9,2,5,1,11, -9, 298)
# Sorting the elements of vector.
sort.result <- sort(x)
print(sort.result)
# Sorting the elements in a reverse order.
revsort.result <- sort(x, decreasing = TRUE)
print(revsort.result)
# Sorting our character vectors.
y <- c("Red","Blue","yellow","violet")
sort.result <- sort(y)
print(sort.result)
```

 # Sort the character vectors in a reverse order.
revsort.result <- sort(x, decreasing = TRUE)
print(revsort.result)

This will give out the following result:

```
[1]  -9   1   2   3   5   9  11 298
[1] 298  11   9   5   3   2   1  -9
[1] "Blue"    "Red"     "violet" "yellow"
[1] 298  11   9   5   3   2   1  -9
```

Chapter 10- Lists

Lists are elements in R which can be used for holding elements of different data types such as strings, numbers, vectors, and even other lists inside it. It is possible for a list to have a matrix or a function as the element. For us to create a list, we use the *"list()"* function.

Creation of a List

Consider the example given below, which shows how lists can be created having vectors, strings, numbers, and logical values:

 # Creating a list having numbers, vectors, strings and logical values.

list_data <- list("Red", "Green", c(20,50,21), TRUE, 61.93, 319.2)

print(list_data)

The program will give the following output once executed:

```
[1] "Red"

[[2]]
[1] "Green"

[[3]]
[1] 20 50 21

[[4]]
[1] TRUE

[[5]]
[1] 61.93

[[6]]
[1] 319.2
```

Naming List Elements

The elements of a list can be given names, and these names can be used for accessing the elements. Consider the example given below, which shows how this can be done in R:

 # Creating a list having a matrix, a vector, and a list.
list_data <- list(c("Jan","Feb","Mar"),
matrix(c(4,7,3,1,-2,8), nrow = 2),

list("green",24.1))
 # Giving names to our elements in our list.
names(list_data) <- c("1st Quarter", "A_Matrix", "A Inner list")
 # Showing the list.
print(list_data)

Execution of the above program will give out the following result:

```
$`1st Quarter`
[1] "Jan" "Feb" "Mar"

$A_Matrix
     [,1] [,2] [,3]
[1,]    4    3   -2
[2,]    7    1    8

$`A Inner list`
$`A Inner list`[[1]]
[1] "green"

$`A Inner list`[[2]]
[1] 24.1
```

Accessing List Elements

We can use the index of the element in the list for the purpose of accessing that element. If the list is named, then we can use the names for the purpose of accessing those elements. Consider the example given below, which shows how this can be done:

```
# Creating a list having a matrix,a vector and a list.
list_data <- list(c("Jan","Feb","Mar"),
matrix(c(3,5,5,0,-2,7), nrow = 2),

  list("green",20.7))
# Giving names to our elements in the list.
names(list_data) <- c("1st Quarter", "A_Matrix", "A
Inner list")
# Accessing the first element of our list.
print(list_data[1])
# Accessing the thrid element. Since it is a list, all the
elements will have to be printed.

print(list_data[3])
# Accessing the list element by use of the name of
element.
print(list_data$A_Matrix)
```

Execution of the above program will give you the following result:

```
$`1st Quarter`
[1] "Jan" "Feb" "Mar"

$`A Inner list`
$`A Inner list`[[1]]
[1] "green"

$`A Inner list`[[2]]
[1] 20.7


      [,1] [,2] [,3]
[1,]    3    5   -2
[2,]    5    0    7
```

Manipulation of the List Elements

The elements of a list can be deleted, updated, or new ones added. The elements can only be added and deleted at the end of the list. However, update can be done to any element of the list. Consider the following example, which demonstrates how this can be done:

```
# Creating a list having a matrix, a vector and a list.
list_data <- list(c("Jan","Feb","Mar"),
matrix(c(3,7,5,9,-2,6), nrow = 2),

  list("green",12.3))
# Giving names to elements in our list.
names(list_data) <- c("1st Quarter", "A_Matrix", "A
Inner list")
# Adding an element at the end of our list.
list_data[4] <- "Our New element"
print(list_data[4])
# Removing the last element.
list_data[4] <- NULL
# Printing our 4th Element.
print(list_data[4])
# Updating our 3rd Element.
list_data[3] <- "The updated element"
print(list_data[3])
```

Execution of the above program should give you the result given below:

```
[[1]]
[1] "Our New element"

$
NULL

$`A Inner list`
[1] "The updated element"
```

Merging Lists

A number of lists can be merged so that we can get a single list. This can be done by placing all the elements inside the *"list()"* function. Consider the example given below, which shows how this can be done:

```
# Creating two lists.
list1 <- list(7,8,9)
list2 <- list("Sun","Mon","Tue")

# Merging our two lists.
merged.list <- c(list1,list2)

# Printing the merged list.
print(merged.list)
```

Execution of the above program should give you the following result:

```
[[1]]
[1]  7


[[2]]
[1]  8


[[3]]
[1]  9


[[4]]
[1]  "Sun"


[[5]]
[1]  "Mon"


[[6]]
```

A list can also be converted into a vector. The elements of our vector can then be used for any further manipulations. This means that with the vector, we can apply any necessary arithmetic operations. For the conversion to be done, we should use the *"unlist()"* function. The function will take the list as the input, and then the conversion will be done to get a vector. Consider the example given below, which demonstrates how this can be done:

 # Creating lists.
list1 <- list(1:6)
print(list1)

list2 <-list(11:15)

```
print(list2)

# Converting the lists into vectors.
vector1 <- unlist(list1)
vector2 <- unlist(list2)

print(vector1)
print(vector2)

# adding the vectors
result <- vector1+vector2
print(result)
```

Execution of the above program will give out the following as the result:

```
[[1]]
[1] 1 2 3 4 5 6

[[1]]
[1] 11 12 13 14 15

[1] 1 2 3 4 5 6
[1] 11 12 13 14 15
[1] 12 14 16 18 20 17
```

Chapter 11- Matrices

In matrices, elements are usually organized in a two-dimensional layout. The elements stored in matrices should be of the same atomic type. Although we are able to create matrices with only logical values or characters, they will not be of much use to us. In most cases, matrices are created with numerical values so that they can be used for numerical calculations.

The following syntax is used for creation of matrices in R:

matrix(data, nrow, ncol, byrow, dimnames)

The following parameters have been used in the above syntax:
1. data- this is the input vector which will become the data elements of our matrix.

2. nrow- this represents the number of rows which are to be created.
3. ncol- this represents the number of columns which are to be created.

4. byrow- this is a logical clue. If it is set to *"true,"* then the elements of the input vector will be arranged by row.

Consider the example given below, which shows how to create a vector with numbers as the input:

 # Elements have been arranged sequentially by the row.
MM <- matrix(c(2:15), nrow = 4, byrow = TRUE)
print(MM)

 # Elements have been arranged sequentially by the column.
NM <- matrix(c(2:15), nrow = 4, byrow = FALSE)
print(NM)

 # Defining the column and the row names.
rownames = c("row1", "row2", "row3", "row4")
columnnames = c("col1", "col2", "col3")

PM <- matrix(c(2:15), nrow = 4, byrow = TRUE,
dimnames = list(rownames, columnnames))
print(PM)

Execution of the above program will give out the following result:

```
       [,1]  [,2]  [,3]  [,4]
[1,]     2     3     4     5
[2,]     6     7     8     9
[3,]    10    11    12    13
[4,]    14    15     2     3
       [,1]  [,2]  [,3]  [,4]
[1,]     2     6    10    14
[2,]     3     7    11    15
[3,]     4     8    12     2
[4,]     5     9    13     3
```

The row and column index can be used for the purpose of accessing the elements of a matrix.

Chapter 12- Arrays

These are the objects which can be used for storage of data in more than one form. Note that only elements of a similar data type can be stored in an array. To create an array in R, we use the "*array()*" function. This will take vectors as the input, and then the values in the "*dim*" parameter will be used for creation of the array.

Consider the example given below, which shows how an array can be created:

```
# Creating two vectors of a varying length.
v1 <- c(4,7,1)
v2 <- c(11,12,13,14,15,16)

# Taking the vectors as the input to our array.
result <- array(c(v1,v2),dim = c(3,3,2))
print(result)
```

Execution of the above program will give out the following as the result:

```
, , 1

     [,1] [,2] [,3]
[1,]   4   11   14
[2,]   7   12   15
[3,]   1   13   16

, , 2

     [,1] [,2] [,3]
[1,]   4   11   14
[2,]   7   12   15
[3,]   1   13   16
```

The parameter *"dimnames"* can be used for the purpose of assigning names to rows, columns, and matrices contained in an array. Consider the example given below, demonstrating how this can be done:

 # Creating two vectors with different lengths.
v1 <- c(4,7,1)
v2 <- c(11,12,13,14,15,16)
column.names <- c("C1","C2","C3")
row.names <- c("ROW1","ROW2","ROW3")
matrix.names <- c("Matrix1","Matrix2")

 # Take the vectors as the input to our array.
result <- array(c(v1,v2),dim = c(3,3,2),dimnames = list(column.names,row.names,

  matrix.names))
print(result)

Execution of the above program will give out the following output:

```
, , Matrix1

    ROW1 ROW2 ROW3
C1     4   11   14
C2     7   12   15
C3     1   13   16

, , Matrix2

    ROW1 ROW2 ROW3
C1     4   11   14
C2     7   12   15
C3     1   13   16
```

Consider the following examples showing how the elements of an array can be accessed:

```r
# Creating two vectors of a different length.
v1 <- c(4,7,1)
v2 <- c(11,12,13,14,15,16)
column.names <- c("C1","C2","C3")
row.names <- c("ROW1","ROW2","ROW3")
matrix.names <- c("Matrix1","Matrix2")

# Take the vectors as the input to our array.
result <- array(c(v1,v2),dim = c(3,3,2),dimnames =
list(column.names,

  row.names, matrix.names))

# Printing the third row of our second matrix of
array.
print(result[3,,2])

# Printing the element in 1st row and 3rd column of
our 1st matrix.

print(result[1,3,1])

# Printing the 2nd Matrix.
print(result[,,2])
```

Execution of the above program will give you the following result:

```
        ROW1 ROW2 ROW3
           1   13   16
        [1] 14
           ROW1 ROW2 ROW3
        C1    4   11   14
        C2    7   12   15
        C3    1   13   16
```

The elements of an array are just organized into matrices in different dimensions. For us to carry out operations on the elements of the array, we have to access them as matrices. Consider the example given below, which demonstrates how this can be done:

```
# Creating two vectors of varying lengths.
v1 <- c(4,7,1)
v2 <- c(11,12,13,14,15,16)

# Take the vectors as the input to our array.
array1 <- array(c(v1,v2),dim = c(3,3,2))

# Creating two vectors of varying lengths.
v3 <- c(9,2,0)
v4 <- c(6,1,12,3,14,3,2,6,7)
array2 <- array(c(v1,v2),dim = c(3,3,2))

# create matrices from the arrays.
matrix1 <- array1[,,2]
matrix2 <- array2[,,2]

# Adding the matrices.
result <- matrix1+matrix2
print(result)
```

Execution of the above program should give you the result given below:

```
     [,1] [,2] [,3]
[1,]    8   22   28
[2,]   14   24   30
[3,]    2   26   32
```

The "*apply()*" function can be used for the purpose of performing calculations across the elements contained in an array. It takes the syntax given below:

apply(x, margin, fun)

The following parameters have been used in the above syntax:
1. x- this is an array.

2. margin- this is the name of the data set which is to be used.

3. fun- this is the function which is to be applied across the elements of our array.

Consider the example given below, which shows how the function can be used in R:

```
# Creating two vectors of varying lengths.
v1 <- c(4,7,1)
v2 <- c(11,12,13,14,15,16)

# Take the vectors as the input to our array.
new.array <- array(c(v1,v2),dim = c(3,3,2))
print(new.array)

# Use the apply for calculation of the sum of rows
across all our matrices.

result <- apply(new.array, c(1), sum)
print(result)
```
Execution of the above program will give you the following result:

```
, , 1

     [,1] [,2] [,3]
[1,]    4   11   14
[2,]    7   12   15
[3,]    1   13   16

, , 2

     [,1] [,2] [,3]
[1,]    4   11   14
[2,]    7   12   15
[3,]    1   13   16

[1] 58 68 60
```

Chapter 13- Factors

Factors are data objects used for the purpose of categorizing data and then storing it under levels. They can be used for the storage of both strings and integers. These are only useful in the columns with a limited number of the unique values. These are good in data analysis and statistical modeling.

For us to create factors in R, we use the *"factor()"* method whereby we take the vector as the input. Consider the example given below, showing how this function can be used:

```
# Creating a vector as the input.
d <-
c("East","West","East","North","North","East","West
","West","West","East","North")

print(d)
print(is.factor(d))

# Applying the factor function.
factor_data <- factor(d)

print(factor_data)
print(is.factor(factor_data))
```

Execution of the program should give the following output:

```
[1] "East"  "West"  "East"  "North" "North" "East"  "West"  "West"  "West"
[10] "East"  "North"
[1] FALSE
[1] East  West  East  North North East  West  West  West  East  North
Levels: East North West
[1] TRUE
```

Once you have created a data frame having a column of text data, R will have to treat the next column as the categorical data and then create factors on it. Consider the example given below, showing how this can be done:

```
# Creating the vectors for the data frame.
```

```
height <- c(140,152,164,137,166,157,112)
weight <- c(38,49,76,54,97,22,30)
gender <-
c("male","male","female","female","male","female","
male")

# Creating the data frame.
input_data <- data.frame(height,weight,gender)
print(input_data)

# Testing if gender column is a factor.
print(is.factor(input_data$gender))

# Printing the gender column to see the levels.
print(input_data$gender)
```

Execution of the program will give you the following as the result:

```
     height weight gender
1      140      38    male
2      152      49    male
3      164      76  female
4      137      54  female
5      166      97    male
6      157      22  female
7      112      30    male
[1] TRUE
[1] male     male    female female male     female male
Levels: female male
```

The order of the levels contained in a factor can be changed by application of the factor function again while specifying the new order of our levels. Consider the example given below, showing how this can be done:

```
d <-
c("East","West","East","North","North","East","West
","West","West","East","North")
```

Creating the factors

```
factor_data <- factor(d)
print(factor_data)
```

Applying the factor function and the required order of our level.

```
new_order_data <- factor(factor_data,levels =
c("East","West","North"))
```

```
print(new_order_data)
```

Execution of the program given below will yield the result given below:

```
[1] East  West  East  North North East  West  West  West  East  North
Levels: East North West
[1] East  West  East  North North East  West  West  West  East  North
Levels: East West North
```

In R, generation of factor levels can be done by use of the *"gl()"* function. The function will take two integers, in which the first integer will specify the number of levels and the number of times for each level. The function takes the syntax given below:

gl(n, k, labels)

The following parameters have been used in the above syntax:
1. n- this is an integer which defines the number of levels.
2. k- this is an integer which specifies the number of replications.
3. labels- this is a vector of labels representing the resulting factor levels.

Consider the example given below, which shows how the function can be used:

vec <- gl(2, 3, labels = c("Texas", "Seattle","Boston"))

print(vec)

Execution of the program will give you the following result:

```
[1] Texas   Texas   Texas   Seattle Seattle Seattle
Levels: Texas Seattle Boston
```

Chapter 14- Data Frames

This is a table or a structure in a two-dimensional format in which each column should have the values for one variable and each row should have one set of the values from each column.

The following characteristics represent a data frame:
1. The names of columns should be non-empty.

2. The names of rows should be unique.

3. The data frame can store data of type numeric, character, or factor type.

4. The number of data items in the columns should be equal.

Consider the following example which best demonstrates this:

```
# Creating the data frame.
emp.data <- data.frame(
  emp_id = c (1:5),
  emp_name =
c("John","Dan","Mercy","Ryan","Joel"),
  salary = c(563.3,589.2,901.0,754.2,803.78),

  start_date = as.Date(c("2014-01-01", "2012-06-28",
"2013-11-30", "2014-05-08",

  "2015-08-27")),
  stringsAsFactors = FALSE
)
# Printing the data frame.
print(emp.data)
```

Execution of the above program will give you the following result:

```
     emp_id emp_name salary start_date
1        1      John 563.30 2014-01-01
2        2       Dan 589.20 2012-06-28
3        3     Mercy 901.00 2013-11-30
4        4      Ryan 754.20 2014-05-08
5        5      Joel 803.78 2015-08-27
```

The *"str()"* function can be used for the purpose of obtaining the structure of a data frame. The example given below best demonstrates how this function can be used in R:

# Creating the data frame.
emp.data <- data.frame(
  emp_id = c (1:5),
  emp_name =
c("John","Dan","Mercy","Ryan","Joel"),
  salary = c(563.3,589.2,901.0,754.2,803.78),

  start_date = as.Date(c("2014-01-01", "2012-06-28",
"2010-11-10","2013-11-30", "2014-05-08")),
  stringsAsFactors = FALSE
)
# Getting the structure of our data frame.
str(emp.data)

Execution of the above program gives the following result:

```
'data.frame':    5 obs. of  4 variables:
 $ emp_id    : int  1 2 3 4 5
 $ emp_name  : chr  "John" "Dan" "Mercy" "Ryan" ...
 $ salary    : num  563 589 901 754 804
 $ start_date: Date, format: "2014-01-01" "2012-06-28" ...
```

We can use the *"summary()"* function for the purpose of obtaining the nature and statistical summary of our data. This is demonstrated in our next example:

# Creating the data frame.
emp.data <- data.frame(

```
  emp_id = c (1:5),
  emp_name =
c("John","Dan","Mercy","Ryan","Joel"),
  salary = c(563.3,589.2,901.0,754.2,803.78),

  start_date = as.Date(c("2014-01-01", "2012-06-28",
"2010-11-10","2013-11-30", "2014-05-08")),

  stringsAsFactors = FALSE
)
# Printing the summary.
print(summary(emp.data))
```

Execution of the above program should give you the result shown below:

```
     emp_id      emp_name             salary          start_date
 Min.    :1   Length:5          Min.    :563.3   Min.    :2010-11-10
 1st Qu.:2   Class :character   1st Qu.:589.2   1st Qu.:2012-06-28
 Median :3   Mode  :character   Median :754.2   Median :2013-11-30
 Mean    :3                     Mean    :722.3   Mean    :2013-02-14
 3rd Qu.:4                      3rd Qu.:803.8   3rd Qu.:2014-01-01
 Max.    :5                     Max.    :901.0   Max.    :2014-05-08
```

Conclusion

We have come to the conclusion of this book. R is a programming language, as it has a number of uses. The language is used for the purpose of modeling data and analyzing statistics in the statistical field. The program is very powerful, as one can use it for the purpose of drawing charts and graphs. These tools are of great importance in the statistical field, and this shows how the language is suitable for its purpose. R is an interpreted language, meaning that works to interpret each line by line.

There are multiple environments which have been setup online, and you can take advantage of these to program from there. With that, you will not be expected to setup any environment on your local machine. However, if you need to program with your own environment, you can download the R setup program which is available for free. You will then have to double click on the downloaded program so that the installation can begin, and it will be easy for you. You will just have to accept the default settings, and the program will be installed correctly. It is after this that you can get into programming.

www.ingramcontent.com/pod-product-compliance
Lightning Source LLC
Chambersburg PA
CBHW070856070326
40690CB00009B/1868